BLACK VOICES ON RACE
AMANDA GORMAN
by Shasta Clinch

FOCUS READERS®
NAVIGATOR

WWW.FOCUSREADERS.COM

Copyright © 2023 by Focus Readers®, Lake Elmo, MN 55042. All rights reserved. No part of this book may be reproduced or utilized in any form or by any means without written permission from the publisher.

Focus Readers is distributed by North Star Editions:
sales@northstareditions.com | 888-417-0195

Produced for Focus Readers by Red Line Editorial.

Content Consultant: Keith D. Leonard, PhD, Associate Professor of Literature, American University

Photographs ©: Richard Shotwell/Invision/AP Images, cover, 1, 21; Shasta Clinch, 2; Shutterstock Images, 4–5, 10, 25; Patrick Semansky/AP Images, 6; Wenn Rights Ltd/Alamy, 8–9; Mary Altaffer/AP Images, 12–13, 14; Damian Dovarganes/AP Images, 16; Chris Pizzello/Invision/AP Images, 18–19; Stuart Ramson/AP Images for UN Foundation/AP Images, 23; Erin Schaff/The New York Times/AP Images, 26–27; Red Line Editorial, 29

Library of Congress Cataloging-in-Publication Data
Names: Clinch, Shasta, author.
Title: Amanda Gorman / by Shasta Clinch.
Description: Lake Elmo, MN : Focus Readers, [2023] | Series: Black voices on race | Includes index. | Audience: Grades 4-6
Identifiers: LCCN 2022000071 (print) | LCCN 2022000072 (ebook) | ISBN 9781637392645 (hardcover) | ISBN 9781637393161 (paperback) | ISBN 9781637394168 (pdf) | ISBN 9781637393680 (ebook)
Subjects: LCSH: Gorman, Amanda, 1998---Juvenile literature. | African American women poets--Biography--Juvenile literature. | Poets, American--21st century--Biography--Juvenile literature. | LCGFT: Biographies.
Classification: LCC PS3607.O59774 Z57 2023 (print) | LCC PS3607.O59774 (ebook) | DDC 811/.6 [B]--dc23/eng/20211104
LC record available at https://lccn.loc.gov/2022000071
LC ebook record available at https://lccn.loc.gov/2022000072

Printed in the United States of America
Mankato, MN
082022

ABOUT THE AUTHOR

Shasta Clinch is a freelance copy editor and proofreader. She lives with her husband and two lovely littles in New Jersey.

TABLE OF CONTENTS

CHAPTER 1
The Hill We Climb 5

CHAPTER 2
Finding Her Voice 9

CHAPTER 3
Taking the Stage 13

CHAPTER 4
Breaking the Rules 19

A CLOSER LOOK
Intersectionality 24

CHAPTER 5
Writing to Serve 27

Focus on Amanda Gorman • 30
Glossary • 31
To Learn More • 32
Index • 32

CHAPTER 1

THE HILL WE CLIMB

The United States had a difficult year in 2020. A deadly virus spread around the world. Many Americans were upset about injustice and inequality. It was also an election year. Americans chose Joe Biden as the next president in a fair process. But some people falsely claimed the election was stolen.

In 2020, Americans throughout the country peacefully protested against racism and police violence against Black people.

Amanda Gorman read her poem in front of US president Joe Biden (front left).

On January 20, 2021, approximately 40 million people watched Biden become president. Near the end of the **inauguration**, a young Black woman read a poem. Her name was Amanda Gorman.

Her poem was called "The Hill We Climb." In it, Gorman said that Americans can come together to heal. People have different beliefs. They have different skin colors. They have different backgrounds. But these differences shouldn't divide people. What is most important is that everyone works together. All the country's troubles are like a big hill. Walking up the hill can be hard. But by working together, people can make it to the top.

Gorman was only 22 years old when she read her poem. She proved that people can have big voices even when they are young. She showed that poetry can be a powerful form of **activism**.

CHAPTER 2

FINDING HER VOICE

Amanda Gorman was born on March 7, 1998, in Los Angeles, California. She was born with speech and hearing **disabilities**. As a result, she struggled to learn to read. But when she learned, she read everything she could. She also started writing stories. In third grade, Amanda learned about poetry.

Amanda Gorman's speech disorder made it hard for her to say "r" sounds. She read poetry out loud to get comfortable with public speaking.

 Amanda read for fun and for study. She practiced writing in styles similar to the authors she read.

Writing poetry let her experiment with words. It helped her better express her ideas.

Reading helped Amanda find her voice as a writer. It helped her decide what to write about. In eighth grade, she read *The Bluest Eye* by Toni Morrison. The book had a Black girl on the cover. Amanda didn't often see books with people who looked like her on the covers. She thought about her own writing. She realized that she didn't write about people who looked like her, either. After that, Amanda promised to always write about the **marginalized**.

THE MARGINALIZED

Discrimination is the unfair treatment of a group of people. It comes in many forms. Racism is when people are mistreated because of their skin color. Ableism is when people are mistreated because of their disabilities. Sexism is when people are mistreated because of their gender. Marginalization pushes groups of people to the edges of society. They are viewed as less important. They have less power in society. They also receive less support.

CHAPTER 3

TAKING THE STAGE

In 2013, Amanda Gorman heard Malala Yousafzai give a speech. Malala was an activist. She worked to promote girls' education. At age 17, Malala won the Nobel Peace Prize for her activism. She was the youngest winner ever. Malala showed Amanda that even young people can make positive change.

Malala Yousafzai spoke to the United Nations Youth Assembly on July 12, 2013. She spoke of education as a key tool against war and poverty.

 United Nations youth delegates make sure their governments know what young people care about.

Inspired by Malala, Amanda became a United Nations youth **delegate** at the age of 16. In this role, Amanda represented the young people of the United States. She spoke to the government about young people's concerns. She also shared her thoughts on global issues.

Meanwhile, Amanda continued to write. She joined a group called WriteGirl. This group encourages girls to believe in their own power. It offers them a supportive community. And it helps girls use their writing to change the world.

Amanda worked hard to combine her poetry and activism. She applied to a program run by Urban Word. This group identifies young people who are writer activists. Amanda's poetry caught the group's attention. In 2014, it named her Los Angeles's first Youth Poet Laureate. A poet laureate's role is to teach others about reading and writing poetry. Amanda started an organization called

 A mural of Gorman appeared in Los Angeles in 2021. The finished mural included a quote from "The Hill We Climb."

One Pen One Page. It offered writing classes for young people in marginalized communities. It encouraged reading. And it helped young people become leaders in social change.

After high school, Gorman went to Harvard University. In 2017, she became the first National Youth Poet Laureate. In this role, she inspired young people to write. Gorman toured the country. She spoke at schools and gave lessons. She taught that words have power.

POET LAUREATE

The United States has had a national poet laureate since 1986. The Library of Congress names the poet laureate. Poets laureate often serve for one year. In 2021, Joy Harjo was given a third year in the role. She was the first American Indian to be poet laureate. Her main project as laureate was called "Living Nations, Living Words." It highlighted the work of 46 other American Indian poets.

CHAPTER 4

BREAKING THE RULES

To Amanda Gorman, poetry resists **conventional** thinking. For her, this is an important difference between poetry and prose. Prose is everyday writing or language. It tends to use complete sentences. These sentences combine to form paragraphs. Also, each line of writing continues to the edge of the page.

Amanda Gorman and actor Morgan Freeman spoke at WE Day California in 2018. At WE Day events, leaders inspire young people to change the world.

Most books are written in prose. News articles are, too.

In contrast, poetry can have a pattern or **rhythm**. Intentional line breaks split up sentences. The breaks help bring attention to certain ideas.

METAPHOR

Poets often use metaphors. A metaphor is a word or phrase that describes something by comparing it to something else. In 2017, Gorman wrote a poem called "The Power of Firsts." In it, she says a girl is "a story waiting to ignite."[1] *Ignite* can mean to set something on fire. Gorman is saying that girls can be powerful. Like stories or ideas, they can set the world on fire.

1. Amanda Gorman. "The Power of Firsts." *She's the First*. Accessed October 28, 2021. http://shesthefirst.org/dayofthegirl2017.

Gorman spoke at the 2018 Incredible Women Gala in Los Angeles. This event honors women's achievements.

Poetry often breaks the rules of prose. For this reason, Gorman believes poetry is a clever way to talk about social change. Social change is the way people work together to improve the world. Through activism, people can break society's rules in a positive way.

For example, in 1960, many restaurants separated Black people and white people. It was illegal for Black people to sit in certain areas. But some Black students sat there anyway. They wanted to build a fairer world.

Activism can take many forms. Boycotting includes refusing to buy something as a form of protest. Writing to lawmakers is another form. People can ask leaders to vote for fairer laws. For Gorman, writing poetry can be a form of activism. For example, she wrote "The Gathering Place." In it, she imagined the world as a village. Its people could work together to solve the world's problems.

Gorman read "The Gathering Place" at the 2017 Social Good Summit in New York City.

Gorman never forgot her promise to speak up for the marginalized. She often wrote about being a Black woman with disabilities. She brought attention to these marginalized experiences.

23

A CLOSER LOOK

INTERSECTIONALITY

Identity is the way people understand themselves. Social identity is based on the groups people belong to. Some examples of social identities are race, gender, and class. But there are more.

A person has many social identities. They affect how that person is treated. They also influence what power that person has in society. Often, people view discrimination through one lens. That lens might be race or gender. But people's social identities all exist at once. The combination of identities shapes people's experiences. This idea is called **intersectionality**.

In "Rise Up as One," Amanda Gorman examines this topic. She explores how acknowledging multiple identities can be a source of strength. The poem says people's differences are worth celebrating. At the same time, people can still find

Intersectionality would say that fighting for only certain women, such as white women, is not enough to make change.

common ground. People can stand as one even with their differences. By doing so, they can speak up together. They can make positive change. And they can make life better for everyone.

25

CHAPTER 5

WRITING TO SERVE

In her poetry, Amanda Gorman often calls on people to work together. This message fit well with the 2021 inauguration. The theme for the event was "America United." The inauguration committee asked Gorman to write and perform a poem. Gorman was the youngest poet to read at a presidential

Amanda Gorman's poem "The Hill We Climb" encouraged Americans to stand together as one.

inauguration. Her reading made her famous. "The Hill We Climb" became very popular. It was even published as a book.

Gorman published other books in 2021 as well. *Call Us What We Carry* is a collection of poems. *Change Sings* is a children's book. In it, a Black girl leads other kids in a song. Together, they change the world in big and small ways.

Many major companies wanted to work with Gorman. They wanted to use her fame to promote their products. In late 2021, Gorman signed with Estée Lauder. The makeup company gave her the title of Global Changemaker. Gorman worked with the company to create Writing

Change. This program promoted reading and writing among women and girls.

Gorman said she wants to be president of the United States someday. A person must be 35 years old to run for president. So, Gorman won't be eligible until 2036. Until then, Gorman will keep writing to make the world a better place.

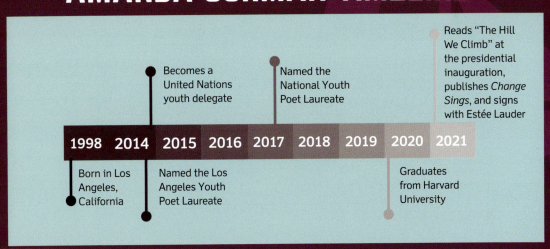

FOCUS ON
AMANDA GORMAN

Write your answers on a separate piece of paper.

1. Write a few sentences summarizing the main ideas of Chapter 4.

2. Do you agree with Amanda Gorman that poetry is an effective way to inspire social change? Why or why not?

3. Which poem did Gorman write?
    - **A.** *The Bluest Eye*
    - **B.** "The Gathering Place"
    - **C.** *Change Sings*

4. How might Gorman's writing about the marginalized be a form of activism?
    - **A.** It lets more people see themselves in the books they read.
    - **B.** It says that white people's experiences are more important.
    - **C.** It keeps the marginalized on the edges of society.

Answer key on page 32.

GLOSSARY

activism
Actions to make social or political changes.

conventional
Following what is normally done or believed.

delegate
A person chosen to speak or act on behalf of others.

disabilities
Conditions of the body or mind that make it harder for a person to do certain activities.

inauguration
An event that officially begins a person's job in government.

intersectionality
How people's multiple social identities, such as race, gender, and class, affect their experiences of discrimination or marginalization.

marginalized
Pushed to the edges of society and treated as less important.

rhythm
In poetry, the mix of short and long phrases to create a certain flow of words.

TO LEARN MORE

BOOKS

Borgert-Spaniol, Megan. *Amanda Gorman*. Minneapolis: Abdo Publishing, 2022.

Latham, Irene, and Charles Waters. *Dictionary for a Better World: Poems, Quotes, and Anecdotes from A to Z*. Minneapolis: Lerner Publishing, 2020.

Schwartz, Heather E. *Malala Yousafzai: Heroic Education Activist*. Minneapolis: Lerner Publishing, 2021.

NOTE TO EDUCATORS

Visit **www.focusreaders.com** to find lesson plans, activities, links, and other resources related to this title.

INDEX

activism, 7, 13, 15, 21–22

Call Us What We Carry, 28
Change Sings, 28–29

disabilities, 9, 11, 23

Estée Lauder, 28–29

"The Gathering Place," 22

Harjo, Joy, 17
"The Hill We Climb," 7, 28–29

inauguration, 6, 27–29
intersectionality, 24–25

marginalized, 11, 16, 23
Morrison, Toni, 10

poet laureate, 15–17, 29
poetry, 6–7, 9–10, 15–17, 19–22, 24, 27–29
"The Power of Firsts," 20
prose, 19–21

"Rise Up as One," 24

United Nations, 14, 29

Yousafzai, Malala, 13–14

Answer Key: 1. Answers will vary; 2. Answers will vary; 3. B; 4. A

32